SONG FOR SARAH

Song for Sarah

Paula D'Arcy

*a young mother's journey
through grief, and beyond*

Harold Shaw Publishers
Wheaton, Illinois

Copyright © 1979 by Paula D'Arcy

All rights reserved. No part of this book may
be reproduced in any manner without written permission
from Harold Shaw Publishers, Box 567, Wheaton, Illinois 60187.

Library of Congress Cataloging in Publication Data

D'Arcy, Paula, 1947-
  A song for Sarah.

  1. Consolation.   2. D'Arcy, Paula, 1947-
I. Title.
BV4907.D37   248'.86   79-14684
ISBN 0-87788-778-0

Printed in the United States of America

for Megan, Max, Michael, Marguerite, Paul
for Peter
and especially for Sarah

ACKNOWLEDGEMENTS

I thank

Meredith Powers, for the use of the poem
on page 7, written for her infant son, Max;

Paul Fanelli, for his photography;

The Robert DeFosse Studio, Farmington,
Connecticut, for film processing;

Sheldon Vanauken, for his personal
encouragement and help;

Donald Kauffman, The Foundation of
Christian Living, who first believed this
Song should be published;

My friends, especially Billy, Ray, Marilyn,
Carolyn, Ann, Bev and Nell;

My family, and Roy's, for their support
which still continues.

Paula D'Arcy

"... I sang him a lullaby,
an unfinished lullaby,
a raspy, whispered lullaby
that made his blue eyes smile."

Meredith Powers

INTRODUCTION

These letters for my daughter, Sarah,
are part of the actual Journal I began in 1973
when I first learned that I was pregnant.
I little guessed then that within two and a
half years they would be my detailed
recollection of a time and a life that was
suddenly and unkindly ended. And yet the
pain and outrage of death eventually
brought me such insight and growth that
these words for Sarah truly became
not a cry, but a song.

Today, three years since the death of my
husband and daughter, I live a full and
warm life with my second child, Beth
Starr, in the same town where Roy, Sarah
and I began our home, still surrounded
by a close community of loving friends. And
yet a real part of our lives will always

be the fact that we are the survivors. Our living is, and will be, an unfinished song—a memory of the life which Roy and I had dreamed of so expectantly, and which we had so briefly begun to share.

So many wonderful people join to make up the memory; together they were a beautiful part of our lives. But the initial dream which allowed these memories was Roy's and mine. And so it should not truly be I alone, but Roy and I together who offer this song: a remembrance of a love and a family which was, for a special moment in time, uniquely ours.

February, 1973

Dear Unborn Child:
Really, dear Andrew, (I'm sure you're
an Andrew. And I am really, truly *pregnant*!
What was just an everyday diagnosis
for a busy obstetrician is a word which
changes my whole life.) I don't know the
words to express my heart's excitement.
Such a joyful secret! Welcome, welcome,
welcome—tiniest baby. Grow strong
inside me.

March, 1973

Dear Andrew:
It's still hard to believe that a "little you"
is really there. Your father is probably
not thinking about you as constantly as I am,
but then you are happening in *this* body, not
his. Still, I notice the way he tells
people that we are "expecting." He's
proud. He's glad of us, and even a bit
incredulous that there will be "you." I don't
know if it's right to say that he's awed
by our news, but he has *some* special feeling
(I see it on his face) as if to him your
coming is almost a miracle.

Your father views us, and everything, as
part of the whole process of life. His mind is
endlessly searching life for answers.
He wonders about the principles which
have motivated man's often
incomprehensible history. But while I
admire his questions, it is not the same for
me. What is real to me is *here*, not a
thousand years ago on some northern plain.
I am moved by this body, which gently
changes to carry another human life. Think
of that! I am almost not able to comprehend
that within me a mind and a soul are
alive, someone separate from myself.

Yet this, for me, is enough. There is no
need to relate us to anyone or anyplace.

I feel little need for the Bible your father
reads from his rocking chair each day. The
stories seem too remote. The essence of
life is surely here. I am sustained by all
our love.

April, 1973

Dear Andrew:
It's beginning to feel like spring. Your
father has started a tray of pepper plants in
our south dining room window. Will I
really eat one some night this coming
winter, while holding onto you? Will you be
real one day?

   Your father and Joe and Pat (What
"uncles" you'll have!) went to Maria's
Luncheonette today for their usual chili.
Your dad said that they talked about
you and the difference you'll make in our
lives. We'll love it when you come.
Together we want you.

   I think that makes a difference. You are
not your father's idea. Or mine. But
ours. We wouldn't think of you without us
all together. A family.

May, 1973

Dear Andrew:
Why can't I look enormous? If you're there
(and the doctor promises that you are)
then I want to look full of you. Everyone
ought to know you're on your way. I
don't appreciate looking just slightly fat.
I want to look positively pregnant.
Poke out, why don't you?
    This night I've begun to sew the casing
for your bassinette. Me, preparing a
room for our baby! I love to walk in your
room. I dream for you.

June, 1973

Dear Andrew:
It's kinda scary, like tempting fate, but I
bought you some clothes today. If I refold
them and hold up each item one more
time for your father's approval, they'll be
worn out before you arrive. Everything
is blue, so I hope you're you! I've stacked
your shirts in little piles, just so.

I've hung your mobile. I smooth the diapers.
I hug the stuffed toys. Then I sit and
look at my belly. I love carrying you.

Your father is working so hard on our first
vegetable garden. He faithfully records
the seeds he plants for future harvest, much
as I record all my first introductions
to you. But I lack your father's patience.
I rush with almost everything. There
is so much restlessness within me. On June 1
your father wrote in his garden record
that "Patience is another harvested food
from the garden; determination another
crop. Bounty comes, if at all, in its own
good time."

I am not in control of this newness about
me. Nature, and the hours, will have their
way.

July, 1973

Dear Andrew:
This morning I patched your father's jeans.
Then just you and I took such a long
walk. We are so close. Your father says I'm
an incurable romantic. Is that why I'm
starting to cry about our shortly never being
so close again? From the second you're
born, you'll begin to pull away and start
your own life. For just a little while longer
it's *us*.

August, 1973

Dear Andrew:
How can I feel two opposites at once?
I don't want this pregnancy ever to be over.
I love living so near you. But when
will it end? I'm so tired. Haven't I been
big-bellied forever?

Our garden is full of crops that want
my care. Two hundred tomatoes tonight—
and all those zucchini to cut off the
vines. And you're in my way, a nuisance to
every chore that needs me. Everything
keeps growing so fast. You too! You can be
so heavy.

September, 1973

Dear Andrew:
The problem is, how am I going to know
when "labor" is real? I will just fold up with
embarrassment if I call the doctor and
I'm wrong. Please, God, strike me with
unmistakable signs so that I can be sure. If
it's all too subtle I'm so afraid I'll miss
my cue. Remember, Lord, I can be awfully
thick.

    And I can be awfully hungry. God, am I
hungry. I never want to see celery or
lettuce again. They only make me hungrier.
My dream is to find a vast bar of chocolate.

October, 1973

Dear Andrew:
This is really the pits. I'm knitting this
little red blanket for you, but I can't
concentrate. I have these cramps, sort of. I
think maybe this is it. But is it?

But then just yesterday the doctor said it
could be a while. Oh, brother. And yet,
if it's *not* labor, then why do I have funny
cramps? I'd give anything to be smart
right now. My grandmother was right about
me all along. No common sense.

Two hours later. Betsy answered my
"Help!" and came over to observe me. Can't
somebody help me decide? "I've had two
kids myself," she says. "If it were
happening to me, I'd know. But this is you.
I can only say you *look* ready. But . . . ."
Pregnant women decide alone.

Well, I'd better call. If it's only abdominal
flu then I'll have to live with it. Thank
God there can only ever be *one* first time.

October, 1973

Dear Andrew:
You're Sarah! I can't believe it! First
we're laughing, then we're crying. We can't
believe it. I *was* right about the labor,
and not with a lot of time to spare! We
laughed, walking into the hospital. I felt so
embarrassed, so obvious with my suitcase.
We kept saying, "This is it!" We laughed till
it hurt—then we worked hard to breathe
you out. The end was so fast—you insistent,
me scared. And your daddy tripping to
get into his delivery room "whites." And
then you. Ten fingers, ten toes, little you.
Perfect you.

Watching you stretch your way into this
world was the fullest joy I've ever known.
Complete. No happiness in my life has
ever been that true. I'll carry your first cry
with me everywhere I go.

Now you suck softly at my breast. I sing
you quiet lullabies. How I love you.

November, 1973

Dear Sarah:
What's happening? Why are you crying?
And why can't I figure out why you're
crying? I thought I was as cool and capable
as they came. But look at me. Who'd
have guessed being a parent wasn't easy?
I love you till I think I'll burst, but
you still get me turned all upside down.
What an adjustment from merely being
someone's daughter to also being
someone's (your!) mother. It's
overwhelming that you depend so totally
on me.

In the hospital motherhood all seemed
adventurous and exciting. But here
at home I'm way too tired to be poetic.
Some days it's a contest to see who cries
more, you or I. How lucky we are that
your daddy is so uncomplaining.

Dear Sarah, do you think we'll make it?

December, 1973

Dear Sarah:
Was I the one who secretly doubted that
one little baby could significantly change
our lives? And so, I had a lot to learn!
We are indeed *very* different with you! The
days that were ours have all become
yours. You first. "Sarah's schedule" has
become the ruling almanac of our week
—or at least of mine.

   Your father's life is a lot less changed.
He is still perpetually reading books and
avoiding the stacks of papers which beg
his correction—an English teacher who
hates to grade! I'd mark the essays
immediately just to get them out of my way,
off my mind. But no piece of paper
creates a pressure upon your daddy's nerves.
It is only I, your mother, who feels
buried by all that needs to be done. One
carton in that cluttered place your
father calls his "study" bears the label
"Student Themes—1972". There they
wait to be mailed. I want to moan every time
I trip over the box. But your father is
wholly unconcerned. It wouldn't ever stop
him from chatting with friends or
watching a rerun of a good Humphrey
Bogart film.

That we might rent his serenity, little
daughter! Let's hope you'll capture
some for your own.

January, 1974

Dear Sarah:
Was I really as harried as those thoughts
I just re-read from November? It seems
so much better now. I mean, I'm far from a
pro, but I do think I'm getting used
to us. Did I often make it hard for you, those
first months? There I was trying to
soothe you with one arm, furiously turning
the pages of my *Dr. Spock* with the
other. I really apologize for being so new
and shaky!

   Please promise me that you'll grow up
and realize that the problem was never my
not loving you. My feelings would
surely explode if I loved you any harder. I
never dreamed what it could be to love
my own child so deeply.

February, 1974

Dear Sarah:
Those early anxious days seem farther and
farther removed now. You and your
father and I have become such a team. Who
could want more than our simple life,
which is so full?

So much began inside of me from the
moment you swelled my belly with love.
You must have sown my first seed of
patience, for I see how I am beginning to
change. I look at my life and I want it
to be good. I want to give away the overflow
of love you and your daddy and I feel.
Some days this house just rings with our
love. And because of the way we feel
about our home, we're planning to baptize
you right here in our living room.
We'll dedicate you to God right in the same
rooms where we eat and laugh and
visit with our friends.

It's hard, Sarah, to lead a Christian life.
The world moves so fast beyond these
simple walls. We're lucky to be sitting here,
waiting for the bread dough to rise,
and to have our big fight of the week be
"who gets the last chocolate chip cookie."
I hope you'll never take it lightly when
we pray with you. Or when we hold you at
the window to watch the birds and squirrels.

Your daddy wrote a poem about us which
says that we three are like a strong
tree with good roots. One of us alone would
be buffeted by the wind. But together
we're strong.

You two nourish me with your love.

March, 1974

Dear Sarah:
Today we spent two hours sitting on the
redwood table blowing bubbles. Me. A year
ago I would have felt too rushed by
my chores and obligations to sit and play
such a game. How you've helped to
slow me down.

   Now I tend all of us as carefully as those
garden seeds we want to grow. I fuss
less about incidental things and care more
about how *people* are affected. I like
to size things up by saying, "In the whole
of my life, does this really matter?"
That helps me to put many silly things aside.

April, 1974

Dear Sarah:
There you are, sleeping just beyond my
door. I get the red badge of courage
today for taking you to your first swimming
lesson at the Y. You looked almost
starved next to the other babies in the
class! I just don't realize how tiny you are
until I see you with others.

How did that water really feel? Do you
have *any* idea what it takes to submerge
a six month old baby? Your father
shook his head at our story. He said he
couldn't even have watched. But you
were a champ! Another of life's beginnings.

While you sleep, your father is in
the basement, busy on a new woodworking
project. Grow up with his temperament,
Sarah. How lovingly he sands the
wood pieces; how patiently he imagines
how he can work them together. I
still sit and look at the jewelry box he
made for me when you were born—so
intricate and perfect. Like you.

Do you sense this harmony of ours? Do
you feel the way we work together?
Are you happy? How fortunate we are,
we three!

May, 1974

Dear Sarah:
My craving for chocolate while I was
pregnant no doubt helped to create the
"hot rod" you are becoming. Sometimes it
takes both your father *and* me just to
hold you flat in order to change a diaper.
How you love to move! You're swimming
so well now. I love going extra times
to give you new chances to flip through that
water. Why did I ever hesitate about
taking you? Let's hope I never hold you
back from anything you want to
do. I only want to enable you to risk, to
dare to try. Such a life you may know!

Will you dream? I dream a lot. I won't
kid you. We *do* live from bill to bill
here, always praying that nothing will break
down. I asked your father tonight if
he thought we'd look back on all our
budgeting someday, and laugh and say,
"Boy, those were the good days!"
He said we might look back, but how could
it ever seem funny?

We laughed. But I wonder. Something
here is so good, even if we're just barely
getting by. I guess it's that *we* are
here. There's joy in that.

June, 1974

Dear Sarah:
Some weeks it's hard to steal even a few
minutes to write. You fill my days. I
have despaired of you ever cutting teeth.
You are so late with them. But you
may creep. At least you are as close to
creeping as you can be without actually
going. And then won't the fun begin!

   I gave your daddy his birthday gift today,
a Gerry back carrier. I can see you two
already, off to explore. He'll have you with
him in the garden, learning to become
an expert at the rows. I can picture you
following him as he cultivates with
his hand plow. He says you were our best
crop of all in 1973. You make our love
even more complete.

June, 1974

Dear Sarah:
Sundays have a different feeling around
here. It's a special day of the week. After
church we spread out the Sunday paper
and your father puts on records from
the Mormon Tabernacle Choir. Then we
read or perhaps continue our ongoing game
of Scrabble. We've been keeping a
running score for months now, and it
really bothers your father that I am winning!
He knows twice as many words as I,
and, in addition, I play with a real
nonchalance. But still the scores show that
I am ahead. We tack our tally sheet to
the refrigerator and the winner of the most
recent match will often boast and
carry on in front of friends. I love the
compassionate, lighthearted rivalry
of our contests.

But it is clearly only in the game of
Scrabble that I have a chance. When your
aunts and I engage your daddy in any
type of a factual question and answer game
we are all losers before we begin.
Your father's recall of any learned data is
instant and complete. He retains the
detail of 14th century English history the
way I have retained only my dress size
and name! He is unbeatable.

Still, we all enjoy one another and have
shared many a long afternoon. I wait
for the day when you will also be an integral
part of our fun. Right now your father
watches you as you wiggle around the floor.
He smiles quietly and coaxes you with
a toy. How we enjoy our simple days and
your growing love!

July, 1974

Dear Sarah:
I'm sitting here at the living room window,
watching the speck of your hat disappear
down the street atop your father's
backpack. My heart wrenches a little that
you have already grown so independent
of me. Yet your love fills me and makes
me glad.
   Did you like that treat last night? Payday.
And feeling rich with his extra
change, your father came home with his
pockets stuffed with tootsie pops.
We laughed, and happily argued for first
choice of flavor. Next year you'll join in.

August, 1974

Dear Sarah:
What heat! Outside is hot. Inside is hotter.
I am amazed that you don't complain.
We have all sorts of fans going, but this
old house seems designed to breed
heat. There's nothing cool to circulate.
    Even in the heat, your father walks
out to check the garden. We've used no
fertilizer or insecticides, but even
so, it prospers. He says that God has spread
his hand over it and thus we'll have
his good bounty.

September, 1974

Dear Sarah:
I never thought of myself in a kitchen
somewhere, part of the community
of mothers everywhere who wash breakfast
dishes to the sounds of Captain Kangaroo.
But here I am—part of the ranks.
How you love the cartoon segments! You
delight in dancing in fantasy with Dancing
Bear. You are so full of wonder at
everything new. And there will be a world
to show you. It's exciting.

   Your father found some swordfish at
a market in Meriden last night. It was $4 a
pound, so he surprised me with three
quarters of a pound, and we savored every
bite! The treat was partly to cheer
me up after a bad day—one of my real
winners. In my usual rush I grabbed
blindly for a detergent bottle and washed
all our clothes with Mop 'n' Glo. I
wonder if I will *ever* change?

October, 1974

Dear Sarah:
In two days you'll be one year old.

Watching you unfold this year has been
the prize for every hard thing I've
ever done. How easily I can now overlook
those first exhausting days (and
nights!). Such memories: our winter walks
with the carriage, with only your
nub of a nose peeking through the soft
stack of blankets; the way you decorated
our house with cheerios (Cheerios
Forever!); watching you swim at the Y,
somehow trusting you to bob to the
surface of the water; and books.

You and your books. We have read books
endlessly, you and I. The same stories, over
and over again. Your father shakes his
head at my patience with you. Patience I
usually lack, but if you ask, I read
the same story five times in a row. And if
you hold up the book again, I start in
for number six. I'm not sure why. Just
something in my heart says that in
"the whole of my life" I may not always
be able to meet your wishes so easily.
But today you're little and it's simple. I
know what you'd like and the supper
dishes will wait. We'll read your story again.

So yes, Sarah, I mean it when I sing
to you that "You're My Best Girl." Even
when you jiggle your musical Bumble
Bee at 6 a.m. and wake me up, I still
overflow loving you.

Happy, Happy Birthday. Number One.

November, 1974

Dear Sarah:
I ache today, but it's not from doing
chores. My sore knee was earned from
continually bending down to "kiss better"
all your bumps and bruises. The
more you learn to do, the greater the
number of accidents seems to grow.
But what a thrill to experience your little
steps. "Out on my own, Mommy! Here
I go!"
    Then, just like me, you invariably trip
over something and hit your head.
Your father laughs and sighs that he'll have
two nuts on his hands now.

December, 1974

Dear Sarah:
It's quiet in the house tonight. Your
father is studying and writing, and you are
far into your dreams. Later your daddy
and I will sit and discuss the ideas he's
considering for the chapters on his
thesis about Tolstoy.

It's funny how differently we approach
things. I am always wondering
about people—what inspires them, what
moves them, what causes them to
hate and love. But your father relates their
actions to *all* life and history,
to the development of the systems of
thought he has studied. Together
our view is that much wider. And I like it
that we share our different
perceptions. I hope we'll always sit up
talking.

January, 1975

Dear Sarah:
What is it that so fascinates you about
clocks? Your aunts were visiting us
this weekend and we laughed at the way
you go crazy when you see one, especially
one that chimes. I bet I have spent
eight hundred hours listening to you
exclaim, "Look! Clock!" over and over,
and then watching you scrutinize the
pendulum if we were lucky enough to find
a Grandfather.
    You and your daddy had a good walk
to Taft School today. It has to be bitterly
cold for us to miss your walk there.
He said that you spent quite some time
trying to get away from your shadow.
Knowing him, he cheered you on!

February, 1975

Dear Sarah:
Will you ever wonder what you were like
when you were sixteen months old?
Well, today we danced magnificently before
the stereo, laughing ourselves into
one another and ending up louder than the
music. Then we walked so far at Taft
School, playing so many games of
peek-a-boo in the bushes that you needed
a "pickup" before we were halfway
home.

    And now, each night before you go to
sleep, I hold you on my lap in the
rocker and sing Rock-A-Bye Baby. You'll
never know how I feel, your curly
head on my chest, as I hear you softly
join in at the end of the lullaby. Your little
notes hug the night air, and are sweet
far beyond my remembering them.

March, 1975

Dear Sarah:
Today you were an imp. I'm trying so
hard to sew you an Easter coat and bonnet,
but when I piece something together
and want you to try it on, you smile and
call, "Pretty, Mommy," and then
fly away! You leave the material flapping
and I can't even adjust one pin. I get
so frustrated. You'll be the only child in
church wearing bias tape and uncut wool!
     But though I tried, I couldn't be stern.
I ended up laughing with you. I can
easily forget, but then you remind me: no
coat is really all that important. We'll
do it some other day.
     Every day is fun for us. You pore over
your books yourself when I'm busy,
and when I sew, you quietly sort your own
basket of ribbons and tape measures
and such. When we play we laugh heartily,
and smile like conspirators at things
only we would know. I like the way we
understand one another.

April, 1975

Dear Sarah:
For someone with very dark Italian looks,
and only one quarter Irish blood, you
surely were festive for St. Patrick's Day.
I thought your green overalls and a tiny
shamrock were a nice enough gesture
to the day. But *you* went on to spill a full
jar of green "sprinkles" for cookie
decoration all over the kitchen floor. Believe
me, when I saw the mess I celebrated
too, and cried in my beer!

   We spend so much time in our kitchen.
It's fun to cook for your father because
there is nothing he doesn't eat and
love. Mealtime here is notably special. And
we doubly love this house with lots
of friends around the table. Our many
friends are a real blessing.

   Your father is already looking forward
to our new garden. We've been out
raking, clearing the leaves and debris. Even
you spend more time in the yard, now
that you're bigger. This year your father
says that the garden will be a family effort.

May, 1975

Dear Sarah:
Not that you'll really care, but constant
repairs are forcing us to sell my beloved
VW convertible. Funny, for you will
never remember it, even though that's how
we went to the hospital for you and
how we proudly brought you home. It will
only be part of a story I'll tell you
someday.

I must be going soft, sitting here thinking
nostalgically about my car. Do you
think it's the sickness? I've had awful
stomach flu and haven't even gotten up to
care for you in two days. That feels
so funny. I am so used to being responsible
for you that it is a struggle to watch
your father take over completely.
Sometimes I lie here, laughing at your
voices. I'm sure the kitchen looks
fire-bombed, and your shirt and pants
haven't matched yet. But I hear you two
chatting along, coming up with some
kind of nourishment three times a day—and
running something that sounds like the
washer. Your father has voiced not a word
of distress, but I do notice he dives

for the bed shortly after you go to sleep.
And I'm here, almost viewing my own
life—sort of stepping back to take a look
at us. Secretly, the rest feels nice.
And we look good.

June, 1975

Dear Sarah:
Your daddy's busy with school work so
much these days. Writing this thesis
on Tolstoy is so important to him. It's
become much more than just an academic
paper required for his advanced
degree. He's really grown to love the man,
having spent so much time questioning
and considering his ideas. At night we
continue to talk together about his
novels. It's so hard to find your own set of
values—your own philosophy.

In the daytime, while your father reads
and studies, you and I play a game
of "Mice." How quiet can we be so that
daddy has a chance to read and think?

Still, he caught us going out for our
walk this morning. "No," he said, he
couldn't come along—"too much to do."
And yet before we had left the yard
he'd taken my hand and joined us. He never
said why he'd changed his mind. And
I didn't have to ask. I'd seen him watch
us. And probably from somewhere our
old promise had surfaced: that we
wouldn't forget that we didn't need to be
rich or important or revered. But we

did need to be together. We said that if
family didn't come first most of the
time, then we'd lose it. You have to work
at family.

Will we always be so fortunate, to
remember that promise? It's so easy to lose
to countless temptations. I pray for us.

July, 1975

Dear Sarah:
Now we know for sure that we live in
*Water*town. What flooding we are
experiencing! We've shed many tears over
our garden. So many plants were
devastated, and the existing squash are
rotting from mold. That culvert which
runs beneath our garden has flooded
everything. And its an irony when you think
of it. For previously it supplied the
secret trickle of water which has been the
heart of our plentiful harvests. But
today the culvert worked for ill. And the
teeming rains have beaten plant after
plant into the ground. We will still harvest,
yes. But the garden will not bear this
time as well as we know it can.

I think we almost feel hurt by nature,
although your father is much more
receptive than I. He accepts the natural
process. Listen to what he put in his
Garden Journal: "These are conditions
beyond a man's control. Wisdom lies
in working earnestly and thoroughly and
not in anguishing over creation's design."

For me, that can be so hard. Even
tonight we sat up late talking about Greg,
your little friend who's been running
a very high fever. I told your father that I

didn't know how Greg's parents stood
it. If *you* were that sick, I *couldn't* stand
it. How would I understand nature? I
have all I can do to write the thought. I fear
I fall far short of trustingly accepting
what I cannot control.

July, 1975

Dear Sarah:
We're visiting your Grandma and Grandpa
in Massachusetts for a few days. You've
told them the secret that has us so
excited: "Mommy's having a baby." Our
family of three—about to be four. Life
is so good!

   True, we never have an extra penny.
Sometimes I wonder if we'll be able to pay
all the bills. We fear that unexpected
expense. But your daddy reads to us from
the Bible. And when I'm sad he reads
me poetry. And so the moments of worrying
pass. We work hard in our garden and
I make our clothes, our cereal and our bread.
Our life is rich in another sense.

   And when we undertake anything—from
a big trip to a new day, we sit down
together first to say a prayer. We never seem
to wind up with any extra, but the ends
always meet. I think we're blessed. God
watches over us.

August, 1975

Dear Sarah:
This summer is bringing such special
moments. We walk together every morning,
exploring the grass, bending over to
look for flowers. I feel so good. One new
child is beginning within me. And
you, our first child, are growing in love.
We watch with pride as you learn and
accomplish so many things. You thrill your
father, clad in your Oshkosh overalls,
running down the garden rows calling out,
"Tomatoes, celery, lettuce...." We
never imagined a little girl who'd know
and love our garden too.

I laugh at the hushed way you excitedly
whisper, "Cherries!" when you
peek into the bag I bring home from the
store. Or the way you eat ice cream
by biting the middle of the cone first. And
who else would sell all her worldly
goods for a bowl of chocolate pudding?

We hadn't planned to do it, but we're
going to take you to Massachusetts
again for a few days. It's so hot, and we want
you to see the ocean. You, who are
thrilled by the tiniest treasure. Whatever
will you think of the great sea?

August, 1975

Dear Sarah:
We were driving home from Grandma's.
You must have been full of memories
of the sand, and the endless holes you and
daddy filled with the sea. Such good
days, but going home always feels best. I
was queasy with morning sickness. Your
daddy reached over and squeezed my
hand. Almost there. You squirmed. I asked
"Would you like a cookie?" and as I
turned around to reach your hand all I knew
was a white car driving at us. My God.

And now, just like nothing, just like the
earth, in a second, can be *not* the earth,
they are telling me, "I'm so sorry."
I'm looking into eyes full of pity and
concern. I hear my voice giving phone
numbers, telling names, reassuring
strangers that I'm all right.

My act must be good. They whisper,
"She's so brave." My mouth goes right
along. I tell them not to worry about me.
"Don't x-ray," I say, "I'm pregnant." Why
is my mouth composed? Roy and Sarah are
badly hurt. Roy and Sarah are dying.

Something hard is happening inside of

me. This *has* to be a dream. How can I make
it a dream? Are you kidding? This can't
be my life. Make it go away. It's a joke.
Horror like this can't find room inside
of me. I don't believe a thing.

August, 1975

Dear Sarah:
This dream is still going on. It won't quit.
Time keeps passing, with or without
me. I've stopped inside, but the outside of
me refuses to recognize that everything
has gone wrong. Just like any other
Monday, any other Tuesday, they bring me
three meals a day. They go on with
their lives. They think the world is
functioning. And I can't take charge to stop
them. I can't even stop me. I'm lost to
myself.

You in another hospital. You, without me,
dying. It cannot get inside of me and
become reality. I cry, but they are not my
tears. I'm no longer me. I'm so far lost. How
could this happen? Who can stop it? It
has got to be stopped. Every muscle and
vein in my body is screeching. Can't they
hear me? This is happening to me and
I can't stop it. I can't make it go away. It
keeps going on in spite of me. How
could this happen?

August, 1975

Dear Sarah:
"Do you understand," they say. They say.
They say, "This is so difficult to ask—but
if she *did* die, would you want her
kidneys to be . . . ." I can't even believe it.
Why am I a patient in this room with
these people in this room saying these
things to me? I'm just about insane and
they're asking me for philosophy.

I won't answer anyone. They'll have
to go away.

August, 1975

Dear Sarah:
I fell apart a bit but it's okay now. You'll
recover. You'll see. It's just a matter
of getting through these bad days. And I'll
help you. I'll help you in every way
I can. We'll be out of these hospitals soon.

Now I'm asking those questions which
have scared me. "Will she have to learn to
walk again?" Don't worry. I've read
about it in magazines. We'll laugh one day
that it seemed like such a big deal.
"Have they cut off her curls for the
surgery?" My little head. But forget it,
because hair grows.

So you see, we're all right. Just that
they've got you apart from your daddy
and me. I can't understand how that could
happen, because we're always together.
How is life allowing this? But not for long.
Your daddy's coma will lift and he'll
help me care for you. We're a family.

Won't somebody go to you and tell you
two I love you?

August, 1975

Dear Sarah:
They said it's over. They said Sarah died
this morning. What do they mean,
"Sarah died this morning?" As if you were
some separate person from me. You
don't die. *You just don't die.* You don't
die without me dying too. Your father
will go crazy. He'll wake up from the coma
and go crazy. We won't be able to go on.
I cannot even believe that this is my life. It's
like a play that won't leave, or stop.

August, 1975

Dear Sarah:
I can't care. I can't care any more what they
come in here and say. The feeling is gone.
They've beaten me. They've won. They
said that your father died. He's dead.
Daddy's dead too. They have ripped my
whole world. There is no more truth
to come. They can't say anything else to me.
Are they glad? Are they satisfied?

I knew that your daddy had died. I knew.
I knew before they came with their
words. I heard him going. But I couldn't
stop him.

Why has God done this? I can't believe
it. Why would he take you both and leave
me here? Why didn't I die too? I don't
want this life. You two are my life.
I just want to die too. How could this
happen?

August, 1975

Dear Sarah:
Wasn't I good enough to die with you?
Am I being punished? I know I am. So many
times I've been foolish, and not really
loving—and now I'll pay. You died because
you were mine and I wasn't good. But
how could a good God be so mean?

I should be back in our garden, or making
custards for supper. But I'm in this
hospital, sending relatives to get your
burial clothes. I'm talking about caskets.
I'm telling everyone that it's all right.
It's *not* all right. Why did you die?
You were only a baby. At least sadness can
never find you now. I'd never want you
to know this.

August, 1975

Dear Sarah:
Where are you? Are you and your daddy
together? Why have you left me here alone
like this? How could this happen?
    What is it like where you are? Is it really
better? How could you two know, and
not tell me? I feel so powerless against this
terrible mistake: I've been left behind.
We go everywhere together, but you two
have chucked me away. I can't change this.
How will I bear it?
    Your daddy used to tease me because I'd
take life so seriously. I was always
meeting people and seeing through them,
feeling their hurts and their sadness.
I wanted to share with them our feelings of
happiness, but was never really sure
how. And your father would make me laugh
at my own intensity. He'd say, "Life is not
easy for you, Paula!" Well what would
he say now? I'll never be the same.

September, 1975

Dear Sarah:
There are constantly people around and
I want to be alone. I've moved in with your
grandparents in Massachusetts because
everybody said I should. I left our home,
our dear rooms, our garden. Everybody
said that I couldn't stay there now. So I did
what they said to do. That's what I do now.

But it's still awful here. I'm in my old
room with my old things—but it's not my
home. I'm not at all who I was when I
used to live here. I'm not who I was one
month ago. I have a memory of that person.
But I don't know how to get her back.

I was so good to you and I loved you so.
Why did you leave me?

September, 1975

Dear Sarah:
I can't be polite to one more visitor. No one
would like me if they knew what I really
was thinking when they say how lucky I am
that I wasn't badly injured. That I
lived. The person I used to be would have
understood their intentions. What *do*
you say to me?

But today I can't pass off the words. This
new person doesn't have energy left to
do anything but stay alive and not scream. I
don't want to hear anyone else's awkward
attempts. They make me angrier than
I already am.

September, 1975

Dear Sarah:
My only consolation is that I have no
regrets. I couldn't have loved you two any
more. Only that makes losing you
imaginable. I've blown lots of things in my
life, but thank God I realized what
I had when I had you. I just never realized
that you could leave.

I want to talk about you. It's all that's
on my mind. I've got to say it over and
over again. I still can't believe it. How could
this happen?

I make everyone feel so uncomfortable.
No one knows how to treat me. I hid in a
store aisle today rather than see an
old friend and watch her get awkward. I'm
always afraid I'll see someone I know
and they'll have to say they're sorry. I'll
never be known for me again. My face
enters a room and I hear everyone thinking—
the tragedy.

September, 1975

Dear Sarah:
Why won't everyone stop trying to protect
me? Or stop trying to be so anxiously
nice? I want to take care of my own life.
(But I don't know how. Will I ever
make a decision again? What did I lose that
my mind won't work?) Why do I do what
anyone says? Did God inflict this sorrow?
Is he angry with me? Did I live through
this for some reason? My mind is so troubled
with questions.

I went home to Connecticut last week,
and friends and family helped me to
empty out our house. It was like tearing
down everything we'd built and denying
that it once was there. It packed us
away as if we'd never happened.

I look at your clothes and your father's
clothes. It's all over now. The worries,
the cares, the events, the occasions.
One day it all ends in clothes and shoes,
deserted in a closet. They make the
worries and ambitions seem so silly. They
laugh out loud at everything superficial
that we let matter. Because one day
everyone's clothes will hang alone in their
closet. And so what was it all for?

If we fuss about our lives—if we make
clothes and houses and work and events of

great importance, then in the end we'll get
fooled. In the end they are so temporary.
There was to be something more.
But I missed it. I counted on tomorrow and
I counted on the two of you. I easily
put off the question of what really matters,
of what gives life meaning, of what is
directing my life. Always so busy.

And now here I am—with plenty of time
—fingering your father's bathrobe and
holding your stuffed Bumble Bee. I'll keep
them both in my closet. I want to
remember what gets left behind until I can
find that *something* which doesn't.

September, 1975

Dear Sarah:
While I was in Connecticut I saw Dr. Audet,
the doctor who delivered you. There
was so much I wanted to say, but tears kept
finding my throat. He was like proof
to me that I hadn't made the rest of my life
up. He remembered that you were true.

I asked him to transfer my records to
Massachusetts and my new life: the outline
of you and your father and all my joy,
reduced to an office card and mailed off in a
manila envelope. Mailing off what once
was.

He was willing to comply, but gently
suggested that he mail only a copy.
"Then if you ever choose to return, I'll
still have all my data right here." The
thought brings tears again, because I
do so want him to deliver this new baby. No
one will ever know. But that doesn't
matter because I've been moved. And so I
can't come back. I could have copies
of my files all over the world, but I've been
moved.

October, 1975

Dear Sarah:
Look at these letters. I can't believe the
hundreds of cards and notes that have
arrived, that keep coming. How I am
blessed, all around, with love. Special
friends, like Judy, say they feel far
away, but they really are quite near. They
can't imagine how strongly I feel them,
and their love.

Students write, and one told that your
daddy "helped show *myself* to
me . . . ." Others tell how often he
spoke of you and me in his classes, of how
he said that his family meant more to
him than life itself, that he would have
chosen nothing different in his life than
our marriage and your birth.

I watched your father look at you so many
times. He had a very special smile for
you, Sarah. How he delighted in you and in
our love. Is he taking care of you still?
I often cry, "Why aren't you here, Roy, to
help me bear this sorrow? Why am I
alone? Why have you both gone at once?"
And though that is true—*both gone*—I
cannot follow that thought for very long,
for it leads to that horrible space where
your father once was.

Your father is gone too. I can say that he
is gone. I can tell someone that Roy

died. But I can't really face the pain beyond
the words. I can hardly think of that now.
It is there, but I have to push it away.
For I am almost overwhelmed just by
trying to face *you* being gone. Other realities
will have to wait for their time.

October, 1975

Dear Sarah:
Tonight I stood outside Nell and Bill Judge's
door. Surprise! Yes, it's really me!
I'm back home in Connecticut—well, for a
little while. Back for some days of
visiting . . . of remembering . . . of trying to
make that life which used to be mine
seem real. As if it *did* happen.

How good it felt to be in their home
those few hours, to be welcomed, as I
needed to be, to talk with their daughter,
Nancy, the babysitter whom you
loved so well. The evening let me pretend
that I was whole again, able to live
on my own. I tried on the life that used to
be mine.

In the preceding two days I'd been all
over town. I rushed to see Dona. I had
supper with the Maxwells. I visited John
and Linda and talked for hours with
dear Glenna and Bob. I wanted to know
about the wedding plans between Pat and
Katie. I looked up Abe. I telephoned
Jean. I felt great energy, and I went on and
on and on.

But ultimately even I couldn't
be fooled. I grew suddenly very tired.
I made such an effort again at the Judge's
door. If they could only infuse me
with their strong love.

But it could not work, my brief
masquerade, for I hadn't the strength to
sustain it. I will drive back to Massachusetts
tomorrow, and now I am very sad.
Their lives have all gone on and mine is
still blown apart. I cannot find me.
I am a name from a memory.

October, 1975

Dear Sarah:
Days and days and days go on. I'm here
going through all the motions, but I'm not
really here. I know I act almost
right, but I'm not right. I'm not fooled
at all. I can never forget, not even
to sleep. I think I'll never sleep. Never
ever again.

And then when a moment of sleep
does come it's no relief but only
more pain. Dreams of you and your
father and this horror. Does this go on
forever?

October, 1975

Dear Sarah:
Hallowe'en. But there is no mask in the
world which can hide me from this
nightmare. I wish there were.

I was thinking today about Dr. Audet. So
many weeks have passed since I saw
him last. But some of his words are just
now repeating loudly in my head.
"If you ever choose to return . . . ." I start,
and I can't believe it. This is honestly
the first time that it has occurred to me that
I *do* have a choice. I mean, I can go
back to Connecticut if I want to. *I can go
anywhere I want to.*

I have choices. I can decide. My life is
still up to me. How could I not know
that? Where have I been? How do I get
myself back?

November, 1975

Dear Sarah:
I thought this pain would leave when I
remembered that I had choices. But
choices make it worse than ever. Choices
don't help at all, because this new
person doesn't know *how* to make choices.
This new person has no skills at all.

I'm sitting here with this open notebook,
facing a page with a line drawn down
the middle. Left side: "Pro—Move back to
Connecticut." Right side: "Con—Stay
here." I have to write all the thoughts down
because I can't hold ideas in my head
anymore. You and your father are all I hold
in my head. And trying to make this
decision is making me crazy. It's too hard.
Making up my mind is too hard for me.
But I'm not like this. Or I wasn't. How can
I not know what I want?

Why do you suppose I am alive? Will I
find out? My life just makes no sense. I am
flooded with questions without answers.
My mind will never be still. Always Roy and
Sarah. Roy and Sarah. That's all I know.

When someone talks I can't really
listen. Never before have I been unable or
unwilling to lend an ear to another's
troubles. But I can't anymore. I'm a madwoman

inside. I'm so saturated with hurt and questions that there's no room for anybody else. There's hardly room for me. How could this happen to me? When will it stop?

November, 1975

Dear Sarah:
Day after day after day I fill out insurance
forms. I sort through carton loads of
your father's papers. It's not fair that I've
been left with all of this. I ought to be
making you a quilt for the winter, not
sorting the boxes of papers piled in this
lousy garage. Every paper, every
scrapbook, every memento of us hurts me.
What would our life be like today if
you were both alive? What would we be
busy with? Might I be sitting in our
living room taking you both for granted,
never guessing that this could happen?

Everyone asks me about the court
decision and about the man who killed
you. They hope that there will be a
big settlement. They want to see him
punished. And what if he is? What if he
is tortured? What if his loss makes
me rich? Neither money nor revenge will
bring you back. There is no victory
for me in a court.

All I'd like is to sleep again. Will I ever
stop having nightmares? At night my
mind makes me face what I don't want to
face: you will never be back.

I still need to talk. I still have to say it
again and again. "We were in a terrible

accident and Roy and Sarah were killed."
Sometimes I catch myself blurting it
out to strangers. I guess in a way that's
easier. I can say it, and a stranger
doesn't try to take my pain. I want to hide
my feeling from anyone who knows me.

Can you understand that? You see, my
feelings are the only thing I have left which
hasn't been wrested from me. My tears
and my pain over you are all I still have
which belongs to the three of us.
Everything else is gone. So even if it does
hurt, it's the last thing I have which
is ours. Everything else in my life is new—
something you're not a part of. I hope
you can see that. These tears are all that's
left of us.

November, 1975

Dear Sarah:
It is bleak today—bleak and bitterly cold.
The day is me. I hate the way I am
angry. I dislike my pain which strikes out
at everyone. I saw a bouquet of flowers
at the store this morning and bought them
for my mother. I feel like I'm so mean to her,
as if she receives my anger just because
she's the one who's most often there. I'd like
the flowers to erase who I am and don't
want to be. They say, "I'm sorry."

People are better to me than I deserve.
My sister Anne gave up her room so that I
could be where I was when I used to
live at home; my sister Bev tirelessly makes
trips anywhere I want to go; her
twin, Barby, encourages me endlessly to
visit, to come for supper, to join her and
her husband at a movie, a play; my
grandmother says again and again, "Is there
anything I can do?"; and the dear
neighbors I call Grandma and Grandpa
Wild, themselves sick, visit me every single
day.

It is nearly a visible support, this circle
of love. With the help of my friend
David and your Uncle Jim I pack away many
of your father's papers and deliver
cartons of his books to libraries or churches.

My dear cousin Nancy drives all the way
from Narragansett every week because
she knows I need someone here. Once we
laughed through Europe together,
thinking a crisis in life was which boy on
the tour to date. Now we eat lunch
together on the piers in Newport, wishing
the sea might tell us what in life allows
such pain. And again and again Betty,
my oldest friend, calls. She listens to me
talk on and on. I repeat the words
about you and your father and our lives. I
talk about going on. I try to make my
life make sense. But it does not make sense.
And I do not talk about the pain I feel,
and the love. I hold that within me. That is
ours.

These loving people most likely do not
know it, but right now they are the structure
which causes my life to go on. They
have become *me*, for a little while, and they
carry on my days until I can catch up
with it all. *If* I catch up. Do any of them
notice that I am gone? I am not even here.

November, 1975

Dear Sarah:
There's a new television program on and
you don't know it. I read something
in the newspaper which would interest your
father and I can't tell him. He'll never
know. Every day new things happen
and I know, but you don't. How can this
be so? How can you be really gone?
Who can I tell the things I shared only
with your father? Who takes care of
me? Who even needs me?

I'm looking at things so differently now.
I used to be so sure of my future. I
was always planning for that future. And
now your father's words repeat in my
head and haunt me: "Life has no
guarantees." There is no guarantee of
anything more than the moment we
have. So if we don't use "today" well, then
we've really got ourselves fooled.

Just think of your father. He was only
33 years old, but he'd asked himself so many
important questions about life. He
wondered about ultimate truth. He sat
every day with the Bible, looking for deeper
understanding. He controlled his life.
He didn't let himself get caught up in petty
tales and gossip; he didn't let himself

rush around so much that a day had no time
for prayer or reading.

And what if he *had* thought that he would
take time for God later, when he was in
his forties or fifties, when his family was
settled, and it was easier to slow his
life down? Then it would have been too late.
The only important questions about
life would not yet have been asked, and he
would have died. Who would believe
that 33 years could be too late? That's our
great delusion.

November, 1975

Dear Sarah:
I get afraid I'll never know where I'm
heading again. Will I ever be a nice person
again? I used to do so much listening,
but that's gone. I'm so full of wanting you
that there's no room inside of me for
anybody else. I can't take anything else in.
When will this stop?

November, 1975

Dear Sarah:
Today did it. I cannot take one more day
of everything being upside down.
A new obstetrician, a new pediatrician, new
stores, new banks, new pharmacies.
Every simple thing I need to do means
asking directions or looking things up.
The outside of my life has become
as strange as the inside of me. How I ache
for something to be familiar.
    And there I was today, crying in the
aisle of the store because I couldn't find
the peanut butter. And then I knew.
I'm getting out of here. I'm going home.

December, 1975

Dear Sarah:
My swollen belly and I are wedged onto a
crate, supervising as they move all of
our memories into this new apartment.
These particular rooms are new, but the
land is home, the streets are home,
my friends are home and my dear doctor is
here. And yes, God, if I go down to
the First National, I'll know just where to find
the peanut butter. That has become my
victory. I must be a crazy woman.

Where would we all be now if the accident
had never taken place? What would
we be like? Could we possibly just be living
normal days, never guessing that one
blink of fate was separating us from this
madness I know?

Do you notice that I never write to you
about this baby? Maybe when my body is at
rest in this place I can finally turn
my mind to him. I know I've been unfair.
I haven't loved and enjoyed his stay
here like I did yours. I don't even know if
I'm able to love someone new. But nature
is keeping its own timetable, regardless of
my consent. And what if I do want
this baby and he dies too? Do you see?

But my time is running out. Soon I'll have
to face all the possibilities. I even

wonder what my sobbing is doing to this
child. I am so sorry. But I'm too
exhausted to make things different. All my
energy goes into not screaming—screaming
forever. There isn't any strength left
over for wanting someone new.

December, 1975

Dear Sarah:
Here I am. But how was the energy ever
found—the strength to make this
move? What enabled me to come back here
to Connecticut and start again? The pain of
choosing to return was its own nightmare.
Yet once resolved, it only became the pain
of saying to my family, who had shown
me so much love and care, that now I must
go off again on my own.

I will ever remember the afternoon I sat
in the living room with your grandpa,
telling him that I was going to leave. It hurt
me to look into all of his love and not
be able to stay. But I knew I had to do this,
for me.

There were fears that he had. He knew
that life could change and be cruel, that I
might return to a memory and find it
wasn't there. His most natural impulse was
to keep me from harm's way. But what
he *would* do, and what he did, were
gratefully not the same. Protection might
have insisted—pleaded that I stay;
instead, love trusted me out into the storm.
If ever I needed his love it was in that
hour. I needed support for the step I was
desperately taking against my own
fear. And he stood behind me, and let go.

He looked at me quietly and said, "I hope
it will all be well." His look was deep,
and our strongest emotions were there.
Then we were silent for a long, long time.
I wanted to hug him, I wanted to cry.
I wanted always to be his little girl. But my
feelings were too strong and I fought
their expression. If I gave into them, maybe
I wouldn't be able to go. And going was
right. And so it ended that there wasn't any
more we could say.

Eventually I left to make some
arrangements and to begin packing some
things in my room. And your grandpa
sat for a while longer in his chair. Then
he left, too. And that night I cried,
alone, knowing that I had caused him the
pain of that goodbye. I never meant
it to be so.

On the morning that I actually left I had
to avoid everyone's eyes. I said, "Well,
you're rid of me. This is it!" Did I sound
brave? For them, I hope so. For in reality I
I had only the strength to shut the car
door and pray to God I could last the three
hours of my journey. I was only sure of
strength to get from one minute to the next.
And I saw every mile of the road through
aching tears. I wept without clear
thought of what I was weeping for. I simply
wept, exhausted and lost. I drove on

because that's what I had decided to do.
I could not resurrect and debate that
choice. There was only energy given to meet
it once.

And so I drove through tears. I wondered
what would be the particular face of
the storm. And finally I looked up to see
that I had arrived, by a miracle,
at my new home.

December, 1975

Dear Sarah:
I look at these boxes that I haven't the
energy to unpack. Look at me. This has
really happened to me. I'm hanging on to
sanity by a thread. My mind holds a
madwoman who can't be shut off. I can't
forget. I see people taking things
for granted and I'm so angry with them
without wanting to be.

Isn't there some way of knowing what
I know without having to go where I've
been?

But how can I be exasperated with
anyone else? Am I any different? Did I ever
value each day? Did I ever ask myself
what in life had lasting meaning, and then
live as though that mattered? I used to
treasure wholesome things, or so I thought.
I felt I had important goals: raising
you, loving our family, extending myself to
others. I put my love for those things
first in my life. And my heart never saw then
that it all wasn't permanent. Even
those good things, when put first, don't
answer what moves the universe, and didn't
sustain me when you were gone.

December, 1975

Dear Sarah:
Christmas. The son of God was born.
God who moves the world; who is the only
thing which hasn't moved. That God
who loved the world. And in this moment
of quiet it occurs to me that he loves
me. I am part of the world. Where has that
thought come from? But it persists. He
never guaranteed anything to be permanent
except his Love. *I* made all the other
conclusions.

I feel some rest. For a time I'm thinking
about Mary and Bethlehem. I've lost
all that I held most dear, and yet my life
need not lose its meaning. Something
says sorrow would have me were it not for
Bethlehem.

January, 1976

Dear Sarah:
A new year. But I don't want anything
new. I want us back together again. My
mind is getting louder and louder. What if
we hadn't stopped for a few minutes
at that gas station? What if I hadn't been
handing you a cookie and you hadn't
been reaching forward? Did it *have* to be?
Was this some nonerasable destiny?
That question won't stop asking itself.

Who or what made these circumstances
that I haven't made? Did you die so young
to fulfill some mysterious purpose?
What purpose? Does God direct every
breath of our lives, and so we are powerless
victims? Or do *we* control our lives
and thus we controlled the circumstances
which put us in just that spot on the
road at the wrong time? If I don't go mad
from sorrow, I'll go mad asking these
questions.

January, 1976

Dear Sarah:
Where are you? Is there really life after
death? Before, that was a neat rhetorical
question. Now it's an overwhelming
enemy. If I could know for sure, maybe it
would ease this tormenting chest
pain. Who would believe that grief could
actually be physical? But the pain is
real. It says that you were alive one minute,
and then I never saw you again. You
see, I'm not writing a story. I'm talking
about *you*. My baby.

Were you scared in that hospital? Did
you think I'd deserted you? I suffer
thinking that you might have believed that,
that you might have wanted me and
thought *Mommy*, but I wasn't there. I cannot
stand that thought.

The most horrible voice deep inside of me
thinks that you don't love me anymore.
Otherwise why would you and your father
have gone off together and left me like this?

These thoughts keep coming upon me
and I can't stand their pain. Why is this
happening? And why now? Shouldn't the
worst have been over many, many
months ago? They all talked about shock.
Could I have been in shock for months?
Is that possible? It was bad then,

but never like this. Have I really been
protected all this time and now the
shelter is slipping away? Can I get it back?
I'm scared. What do I do? I will never
make it through day after day of this. I'm
seeing and feeling what I don't want
to know. I'm looking straight into that
horrible space between us, and I will never
make it.

Do you think if I just let go and cry it all
out then one day the tears will stop?
What if I never stop crying? They're all out
there telling one another that I have
such courage. And here I am—so very, very
scared.

In September someone sent me a booklet
of Norman Vincent Peale's, and
I read it over for the second time today.
He said that with the help of God
nothing can ever destroy or defeat you.
That is the only hope I have. All I've
got left is a prayer that what he said is true.

January, 1976

Dear Sarah:
I'm still pretending for others. How I wish
I could pretend for myself. Just
when I felt myself beginning to do well,
I'm falling apart. But at least no one
knows. When I have to go out, I get all
dressed up and I smile. I think I do
well. The worse I feel, the better I try to
perform in public.

I'm not trying to be dishonest. I just don't
want to let anyone know how badly off
I am. You are *my* loves, and this is *my* grief.
And I do think I've got almost everyone
fooled. They think my mourning is
over now. They no longer ask how I'm
doing. They figure enough time has
passed . . . and I don't blame them. I used to
think grief went away quickly too.

They try so hard to "involve" me again.
They're inviting me here and there.
They look at my face and they assume it's
me. They feel that I can do things again.
They're ready for me to be well. But
their conversation, their attempts, are all
bouncing off this crazy mind. I'm not
me. I'm cracking up.

Day after day I take the phone off the
hook, lock my door and cry. Hour upon
hour the tears come. I want you, I need you,

and I can't get over it. I can't accept it.
It's this despair of being left. It's this
incredible chest pain which says I can't have
my baby or my husband. Me moaning?
Wasn't I too controlled for that? But I've
lost those controls. I'm just crying and
crying and crying.

I'd give anything. I'd accept you ill and
nurse you for a hundred years. I'd take
you in an endless coma. I'd even see you and
then leave you again. *But just to see you
once more.*

February, 1976

Dear Sarah:
"You're so brave." How many times will
someone tell me that I'm so brave?
I stand at the window watching the snow
fall. Tears wrack my huge belly. I don't
want this thought, but it persists:
My baby's in that ground. That chilly
ground. What if you're cold?

This isn't brave. This is a lady whose
mind just won't shut up. I pray and pray to
find a way out. But even so I'm cracking
up. Maybe it's a good thing that I pretend
in public. Those performances are my
only relationship to sanity.

Then this baby. My body is preparing to
have a baby. And everyone talks about this
baby as if it is their answer to my
sorrow. But it's not *my* answer. This baby
is someone else, and it won't change
the fact that you are gone. You are still dead.

My friend Carolyn goes weekly with me to
the LaMaze childbirth classes. I feel like such
a sight. Everyone else has a husband,
as it should be. And then there sit Carolyn
and I. It is all wrong. I hate it. "Is
this your first child?" they ask. "No,
second." "Oh, then how old is your first?"
Over and over again.

I am exhausted. I'm so afraid I'll crack

up. Life outside of my mind doesn't even
exist for me anymore. You're the only
thing that's real, and then sometimes even
you seem unreal. Like I dreamed
you both. I try and can't remember your
faces. That hurts more than everything else.
   I'm hardly living "real" life anymore.
I'm skimming the surface. I'm alone.
My initiative has died with everything else.
I see that I am loved. That *is* getting
through. I'm blessed with friends and
family. I know they're aching to help me,
but I can't ask. I can't let them. This
pain is ours and not anybody else's. I let go
of this and you're gone. Do you see?

February, 1976

Dear Sarah:
How easy it was to have what I called
"faith" in our old life, with our walls full
of love and our future full of promise.
How easy, like loving someone who's only
gentle and good. But this is hard faith now.
I still hear myself praying, but the
faith cannot erase the pain. How hard it is
to believe that I am not alone with all
this hurt. How hard it is to believe that there
can be a victory the other side of these
tears. But that is Christ's promise. And I do
believe in the power of his words:
"Whosoever . . . shall not doubt in his heart,
but shall believe that those things
which he saith shall come to pass; he shall
have whatsoever he saith." I pray to find a
way out of this. I want to get through
it all.

February, 1976

Dear Sarah:
Something happened yesterday. I am still
quite struck. I had dinner with
Carolyn's family, and tried to chat happily
with her children. It was an evening
similar to many we have shared. But the
following morning their eleven year
old son, Joe, totally unbidden by any adult,
did an incredible thing. He approached
Father Jim, the priest for whom he is an altar
boy, and asked him to please see a friend
of his whom he felt needed some help. Me.
That friend was me.

And so the priest has called, and I was so
shocked I said yes. Yes, I am going for
help. Yes. How could a young child arrange
for me what I couldn't do for myself?
How could a young child know? I only know
that deep within me, I guess I am
glad. This pressure of holding on to you has
become much too hard. I don't want to go
mad. So don't be angry if I talk about us
finally. You know I treasure all that we are.
But maybe we have to part. I never
thought it would come in this way . . . but
maybe this is an answer to my prayer.

February, 1976

Dear Sarah:
You—you who've heard everything—you
may not believe it; but Father Jim said that
the way I am is normal! All of it. All
this craziness—normal. *Normal!* I may not
be a madwoman. In fact, one day I *could*
be me again. I know that right now that's
just an idea. But it's such a strong,
positive one.

   Do you understand? I could keep having
these awful moments of remembering
you both, and even think that I won't live
past the pain. And still one day I could
find that it is better. That I'm all right. It's
the strongest hope I've had. I might be
me again!

   Please don't resent it if I do recover.
Don't resent it if I want this new baby. I
think I do. I think I dare to love again.
"We" won't change because of that. Even if
I go on, we will always be a part of me,
a memory of our days together. Nothing
touches that. Nothing ever touches that.

February, 1976

Dear Sarah:
I search through literature and through
Scripture. I talk to people. I'm
still looking for answers. If only there
were easy answers. God loves me. I keep
beginning there. And I don't think he
watched you riding down the highway
and said, "Let's kill her." He loved you too.
So then *why?* Why did it happen?

One moment the anger is gone. Then it's
back. The pain ceases. It returns. I thought
it was possible to reach the saturation
point and finally account for all the sadness.
But life's not so neat.

March, 1976

Dear Sarah:
My baby is so overdue. I feel tortured,
waiting like this. What if the accident
damaged him after all? What if he dies, now
that I realize that I want him? Could
I stand it? Could I love someone else and
lose them? I could never stand anyone
else dying.

    If I didn't need my phone to call the doctor
I'd rip it out. I hate it. It rings with
everyone's concern. It rings with
possibilities I don't want to face. It reminds
me how scared I am. Why aren't I me
yet? What if I come this close to coming
back, and then don't make it all the way?

    God, do you ever weep with me?
Don't you see the goodness that was
thwarted because one man drank too much
and hit us with his speeding car,
and didn't care? Does that man ever think
about me, or wonder about Roy and Sarah?

March, 1976

Dear Sarah:
I have lived forever with questions. But
slowly some answers are beginning to
unfold in my heart. It's no miracle or sudden
revelation. But I am beginning to see
some things. How I pray to see.

I think part of the *why* our accident
happened has to do with all men being free.
All men are free to think and act and
make their own choices. And all the choices
have consequences—results which
fall into the lives of the many others with
whom we live. Think of it! And so it
was possible that a man drank and raced
his car on the highway. His choice. And we
were driving home. That choice was
ours. And we entered one another's lives
in a terrible manner.

Do you see it too? Just one man, motivated
by greed or pride or desperation may
choose unwisely and jeopardize the good
toward which others may have been
striving. Man is not perfect. And a free
choice may be good or bad. That leaves
man with a tremendous potential. A
frightening one. That leaves man as a
channel of light, or a party to darkness.
There's no way *not* to choose.

God did not finger you to die. Rather,

nature had its way. Nature and man, neither
perfect. But all of us subject to the
processes they set in motion. How guilty am
I? What have my many thoughtless acts
set in motion? How many times have I done
nothing and so abetted the darkness?
How responsible man is to this life.

And God. Where is he? He changes
neither the acts of nature nor of man. We
remain free. He created us free, and
with that terrible freedom we live. But the
moment we prefer the Light, he transforms
. . . he transforms not the circumstances,
which we create—he transforms *us*.

He transforms how we see what has been
there all along. It never changes. We do.

March, 1976

Dear Sarah:
You have a little sister and I've named her
Beth Starr. Can you see her sleeping
here? Do you watch us, and smile?

Please, God, don't let her die. Don't let
my sisters or parents or anybody die. I
couldn't stand it yet. But Beth is here and
safe right now. Hundreds of people have
wished us well, and have perhaps thought
that now things are okay. I wish it
were that easy. But Beth is head to toe
memories of you. Memories of how your
father and I shared you. And now there's no
family. Just me, and a baby. Will I be
able to go on?

Only today have I realized that I am not
the only one who grieved. How could
I not have known that? Our friends, our
families—so many felt the loss. Your
father's parents lost a child too. But it all
escaped me. I have been so far away.

March, 1976

Dear Sarah:
Everyone dies. I mean, no one lives forever.
So then why do we live? What is it all
for? How easy to focus alternately on either
our joys or our tears, as I have done.
We get caught measuring life that way.

Your father was right all along. Life is far
deeper than one man's particular existence
in a given town. How blind I was! History
has played out my story against hundreds
of backdrops. And though they were
important to the individual lives, none of
the brief joys and tears have ultimate
meaning. Pain would defeat men if it did.

No, all those circumstances around
which I measured my life were
impermanent. How tempting to believe
they were of lasting importance.
I acted as if that were so. I let them shape
my days. I was easily fooled. They
were wonderful and to be cherished only
within perspective. As life's final
priority, they were false.

All those moments hung one day in the
same closet with your empty clothes.
The best of them eventually passed. They
moved. All that remains, from all that
we were, is the love. And Jesus said,
"I am the Light of the world." The Light of

the world is Love. God, Love, did not
move and does not change. So the question
in life, every day, for every person,
is not what can I enjoy, or who will I please,
or how do I look, or what can I do or
achieve. The question is, how do I love? Am
I a channel for the Light?

I am sure of one thing, my little one.
Emptiness is all around us. But if one
chooses to look for God, he will not
be empty and his life will never be the same.
Christ has promised that. And no man
avoids that choice, for to ignore it is to
decide.

April, 1976

Dear Sarah:
Easter. Look at Calvary. I think I
understand it now. Sorrow was even a part
of Christ's life. And he didn't remove
it because sorrow and joy, together, are
facts of our humanness. He knew.

I've feared sorrow and tried to pursue
joy. I thought that God ought to
prevent all tears. I never realized what it
implied when I believed that man's
choice is free. God has not sent me these
tears. These tears, I finally see, are his
same tears from Gethsemane. These
tears are man's.

April, 1976

Dear Sarah:
Bit by bit I am able to face the memories,
my remembrances of you and your father.
I take them out slowly, when I am able, and
go over them one at a time. Some
moments seem now so distant that they
might almost have belonged to another life.

I am sorry that you'll never know me
any better, or see me any other way than as
a shaky new mother and a young wife.
There was more we might have been if your
life had gone on. There was more for
you to know. I'd like you to have seen me
with your father and his proudest
purchase, a BMW motorcycle. What trips
we took with that bike, the two of us!
How I loved my arms about your father,
trees and mountains speeding by!
What a sense of being free.

I remember the day we climbed the dirt
trail that grew too steep. Our beloved bike
tipped for the first time, spilling us,
rather startled, onto the bumpy ground. We
laughed, aching, on the grass—and then
righted ourselves and were off again,
being from that point on much more
respectful of dirt and inclines. We sailed

into the wind, passing out the miles to
the day, and it seemed that nothing could
catch us or harm us. What would?

I dreamed a million dreams, riding along,
whispering them onto the lips of the
wind. I dreamed us in a thousand different
ways. And I hugged your father and
loved our freedom and the sun, our flights
into spring—our joyful flights. And
now the pain that we won't be sailing the
highways any longer. The pain bred of
our love, which was taken away.

One day I longed to pretend that Beth
was you, just for one day. Just to have you
that one last time. But I couldn't let
me do it. You're gone, and it is over.

Then I searched today for our old lawn
mower. What did I do with it? I visit friends
and see some of our things in their homes.
I must have given things away. I don't even
remember. I was so far away.

April, 1976

Dear Sarah:
Some days in one's memory are forever
vivid, regardless of the passage of time.
And I will always know the sounds
and will feel and sense every impression
that was real to me on the day they
said that you had died.
    I face that moment today: my friend
Carolyn standing there, holding
my hand, tears streaming down her face as
the doctor spoke. "Your daughter
has gone." For a while we stared without
thought, Carolyn, just by her
presence, holding onto the parts of my life
that were now too terrible for me
to bear. Then one by one the faces of my
family and your daddy's family were
all around the bed in that eternal hospital
room. Pain lived with us all.
    A kindly nurse, with long, dark hair,
walked quietly in and out, unsure of how to
face my nightmare. There was a gentleness
about her. Trays arrived with food.
Flowers. Presents which could not erase the
way life had reached out to wound. I
was never, perhaps, more vulnerable than
in those hours . . . and I never felt more
betrayed.
    Time continued without my knowing or

caring that it had. And later in the day
I looked up to see Rick, a friend from a time
very long ago. Rick had been my close
companion in college years, and we'd
shared a friendship of a very special kind.
He had been a part of my happiest days.
We drank beer together, laughed about
classes and filled up the emptiness
of many long weekends at school.
Professors at graduation couldn't believe
we weren't to be married, and we
grinned that they could have thought it so.
For ours was not a romance, but a
friendship. A unique friendship. Probably
a gift.

But years had passed since those carefree
days, and now I knew I was not ever to be
carefree again. And yet at the
precise moment of an agony I couldn't
understand, there was the friend I needed.
How did he know to come? What impulse
prompted him, upon hearing of our crash,
to leave work and drive to be at my side?

But the questions come from now. They
weren't the thoughts I had then.
Then there were no words between us, only
tears and his holding my hands . . . my
hands which didn't have life. He found my
terror and protected me from it, for a
while. I was not ready then.

Always that day will include the people

and the sounds of those hours. All the
life was gone from me, although I could
not, as I wanted to, die. Life kept on. Others
were there. And though I could not see
it . . . it was true that love was surviving
the loss and enduring the pain. From
the first terrible moments, I never realized
more that I could stand. There was never
more than I could bear. Someone, never
moving, knew me . . . and did not cease to
hold me and care.

May, 1976

Dear Sarah:
What kind of future will I offer Beth?
What kind of future will there be for me?
I stand by the window watching our
neighbors visiting with their families on
Sunday. Weekends are no different than
weeks for me anymore. Beth and I are so
rootless. We don't belong anywhere.
I feel like a lady, any lady, living with her
baby. Period. Nothing defines us. I walk
Beth in her carriage and hate the homes with
yards and clotheslines and fathers.
There still are moments when I hate my life.
It hurts.

But slowly my peace within grows. Can
you understand that I still suffer over you
and yet I am finding a way beyond it?
There is pain and there may always be pain
—but it no longer defeats me. I can go
on. God's Light transcends human
suffering. The hope I clung to is strong
and real.

June, 1976

Dear Sarah:
For so long I wished Beth could be you in a
thousand different ways. But I've
separated you now. I really love her for
herself. I think you would love her too.
She's very gentle and smiles at little
things and seems touched by a special love
from all we have come through together.
    Don't feel betrayed by our happiness.
I love you both. But I don't say any longer
"If Sarah were alive", or "If Roy
were here . . . ." You two are gone. Beth and
I are the survivors. We go on.
    I've held on to you so hard.

July, 1976

Dear Sarah:
I'm doing well. Your deaths are always
there, but I'm integrating a lot better now.
No more act. No more standing outside
of life, looking in. You are always just
beyond my conscious thoughts, but I
realize that may be so for a long while.
Now I can accept that and go on.
    I've been thinking. I bet you're longing
for the day when I'm completely me
again all the time; when I can write to you
like I used to, of full and good times.
But then it occurs to me that if that day
arrives, then there won't be any letter.
Or not a letter to you. Do you understand?

July, 1976

Dear Sarah:
I almost bought a house today. When the
owner refused my first bid and wanted
to negotiate, I came to, with a start.
What in the world was I doing? I didn't
even like the house, and it was far too
much money.

But I knew. It was my last attempt to run.
That final desperate chance that if I changed
my life fast, and found someplace new,
then I still wouldn't have to suffer over you,
that I could move away and leave the
sorrow.

But this time at least I see hope. Because
I did eventually catch myself. I caught
myself in the same way the "old me" might
have done before. I think I'm finally
coming around. Somewhere in the near
distance I see *me*.

August, 1976

Dear Sarah:
We are all so powerful. You and I and
everyone. Our words and our thoughts,
which cause our actions, generate so
much power in the cosmos. Really, not only
the big choices but even the little ones
matter—because through all of our
choices we set so much in motion. What
great waves we generate via our beliefs!
Then how important it is that we care
about the direction of our lives.

I sat on my porch today feeling lonely.
And as my mind wandered, I imagined
that I had lived at the time of Christ. How
lucky that would have been, I thought.
Even loneliness would have seemed easier
in his company.

And then it struck me and was so real:
Christ *does* live, and we *do* live in the same
time. No wishing and no "if only."
Christ does live and his Love is here. He
alone has never moved. That's the
statement of the Resurrection. Nothing dies
and nothing ends. When we reach one
conclusion we only become part of another
beginning. Your father wrote it in
his Garden Log: "Every seed has its Easter."
Now, finally, I understand.

August, 1976

Dear Sarah:
I will never be exactly the same, but I know
I am ready to go on. Even though our
love stretches beyond any grave, my life here is
without you. You've become the seed of a new
beginning, somewhere I've yet to know.
I still cry for you and your daddy, and maybe
that will always be so. Some days and
some times may always bring tears. I understand
and accept that as part of love. But can
you see what I'm trying to say? I'm saying
goodbye.

Do you remember, from our trip to the
ocean, the way the water held the sunlight in
the morning? It contained it, and yet
never possessed it for its own. I will always
hold you as the ocean holds the sunlight.
I hold the lullaby we sang together, your voice
so little and clear. So say a prayer for me.
As I say one for you. And let me go.

January, 1979

Dear Sarah:
I visited you at the cemetery today. Well,
not really you, *in fact*, but the you of my
heart. I rarely make the trip to that site,
for I know you are not to be found
there. But still, our last ritual on earth
together was the ceremony at that grave.
   Now you and your father have journeys
I know little of. And when I think of you
sometimes, remembering, I visit your
ground and leave you violets—a bouquet to
the best of our memories, to the moments
which will always smile. I think of all
that has become of our lives, and though,
seemingly, I should feel more fragile,
it is only a new strength I am sensing.
   I look at what I wrote on your grave
marker: "The Lord is My Shepherd, I Shall
Not Want." How well I realize now that
that is true. Even though, through our free
wills, *we* do all the choosing—allowing
life and controlling it, overall, is the Hand of
the Shepherd. Always, for me, at every
moment, he was there—there when I felt his
presence, and equally there when it
seemed I was all alone. His presence did
not depend upon my "feeling" it, or even
upon the extent of my belief. God was

simply there. He did not move, as I realized
that first Christmas after losing you.

Also, ironically, neither pain nor
happiness were true indicators that he was
or was not there, though often I mistakenly
thought that too. His purposes work
together in *all* conditions of life, if we
could only see. Maybe you know all that
now. You know much more than I. For even
in affliction was love—love even in my
tears.

I ached and sorrowed so at losing you.
But the pain, in the end, did not have
the final say. And so it was all much less
a loss than a victory. For Love has
the final say—"The Lord is my Shepherd,
I shall not want." And we are all quite safe.

E P I L O G U E — *Letter to a Friend*

Dear Van:
On the 11th of January, 1979 I had a dream
-vision that I should like to share with you.
I will never know if it was from God.
I do know it was startlingly real. I was in
some house I cannot place, in the early
morning, caring for Beth in the kitchen. I
went up to my bedroom to dress, and as
I changed I looked up and there was Roy in
the hallway, stepping from the bathroom,
brushing his teeth. It was as normal
as pie, him in his underwear . . . an early
morning scene. It was so much he that he
began goofing around in a way that
was familiar only to us.

My initial thought was, "He's dead . . .
how can he be here brushing his teeth?"

I never ran to him. We didn't speak. We only
motioned and laughed as we did when
we expected years and years to stretch
before us. I noted that he'd put on weight.
At the time of his death he had been
lamenting that my cooking was encouraging
a pot belly. And I thought to myself,
how could he gain weight in heaven? Isn't
everything perfect there? He went
back to the bathroom and his teeth. I
finished dressing, wondering if his
naturalness and our remembered joke were
meant to convey to me that he was
still the same, still essentially Roy—that the
personality characteristics weren't
diminished or changed. The weight gain?
A puzzle.

I went downstairs and sat at the dining
room table. Roy came down and went all
around the house with tools, checking
things out. Finally he came to me and
said that he could see that I needed him.
There were things to be done that I
couldn't do. I asked, "Will you help me?"
but he shook his head and said, "I can't."
I understood at that point that he was
aware of my life . . . but couldn't intervene.

He sat down then, opposite me at the
table. Of all the things I've often said I
would ask him if I only had the chance . . . I

never said a word. But when he spoke,
it was the one thing (I thought afterwards)
that I probably *needed* to hear more
than anything else. He told me that he was
sorry. That he never intended to leave me.
That he loved me, but had had to go.
Again I was startled because he was
genuinely sad. I could see that. And I
thought to myself, isn't heaven only happy?
I thought only the living grieved. But
it was clear that it had affected him too,
that he had been aware of my pain, but
couldn't prevent it. We touched then for the
first time—just our hands across the
table. I felt aware that we had to be sitting
there on borrowed time. But still I never
spoke or questioned.

What we did for those few minutes was
grieve *together* over the wreck of our family—
the only time my grief was shared. I was
so aware of Roy's sense of powerlessness to
help me. He said quietly, "At least now
you don't have to struggle. You have
money." And no sooner had he said the
words than I cried and then he did too. The
money is the emptiest gain of the whole
affair. We sat a while longer with our tears,
and then his presence was gone.

I thought to myself, now I'll go back to
sleep, and was drifting that way when
my telephone rang. The call was from a

friend who *never* calls at 6:50 a.m. and he
had no clear reason for the call. An
impulse. I was annoyed at first, thinking
the dream might have gone on. But having
been awakened I began to write my
memories down. Afterwards I wondered if
I would ever have recalled it all if I had
not been immediately roused. Who knows?

As I asked at the start, was it merely a
dream? Was it a reality? And *if* a reality,
then I am struck anew that Roy, having
died, is grieving. How I have wondered
about the true extent of his commitment to
Christ, for I really didn't know if Christ,
for him was *first*. And if not, then maybe
there is still much work for him to do.
Much internal work. It is a hard question.

At any rate, I've shared this with you,
as I wanted to. And now I am packing up
Song For Sarah and going off to bed. Thank
you for listening to me well into this night.

                                    With love, Paula.

Roy, Sarah (9 months), Paula

Our home in Watertown

Roy in his garden . . .

. . . and canning the produce

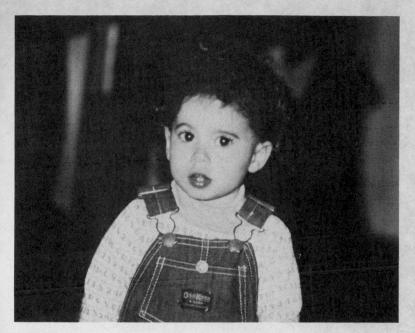

Sarah, just before the accident

Paula with Beth Starr